Our **WILD**™ **WORLD** SERIES

Moose

NORTHWORD PRESS
Chanhassen, Minnesota

DEDICATION
For Ryan Andrew Ohl—may his world be filled with high adventure and grand discoveries

Photography © 2000: Robin Brandt: front cover, pp. 14, 20-21, 27; Craig Brandt: pp. 4, 12-13, 43; Donald M. Jones: pp. 5, 10, 30-31; Michael H. Francis: pp. 7, 8-9, 17, 28, 36, 37, 44; Robert McCaw: p. 18; Howie Garber/www.wanderlustimages.com: p. 19; Mark Wallner/Wing It Wildlife: p. 22; David A. Murray: pp. 24-25; Tom & Pat Leeson: p. 40; Lisa & Mike Husar/Team Husar: back cover, pp. 34-35, 39.

Illustrations by John F. McGee
Designed by Russell S. Kuepper
Edited by Barbara K. Harold

NorthWord Press
18705 Lake Drive East
Chanhassen, MN 55317
1-800-328-3895
www.northwordpress.com

Library of Congress Cataloging-in-Publication Data

Fredericks, Anthony D.
  Moose / by Anthony D. Fredericks ; illustrations by John F. McGee.
    p. cm. -- (Our wild world series)
  Summary: Discusses the physical characteristics, habitat, behavior, and life cycle of the moose, whose appearance hides strength, speed, and agility.
  ISBN 1-55971-744-0 (sc)
    1. Moose--Juvenile literature. [1. Moose.] I. McGee, John F., ill.   II. Title.   III. Series.
QL737.U55 F72 2000
599.65'7—dc21   00-028161

Printed in Malaysia

10 9 8 7 6 5 4

Moose

Anthony D. Fredericks
Illustrations by John F. McGee

NorthWord Press
Chanhassen, Minnesota

WHAT IS THE world's strangest-looking animal? Is it the giraffe with its long neck? Is it the raccoon with its striped tail and black face mask? Or is it the elephant with its long trunk? All those animals certainly are unusual. But many people think the strangest-looking animal is the moose.

At first glance you might think that big mistakes were made with the moose. In fact, some people say that a moose looks as if it had been put together with parts of other animals.

For example, a moose has a short tail like a deer. It has a beard hanging from its chin like a turkey, and big ears like a burro. It has four skinny legs like a horse, large shoulder humps like a bear, and a stomach with four chambers like a cow.

A moose's long nose is sometimes called a snout, or a moose "muffle."

This young moose stays close to its mother, wherever she goes.

Moose have been around for millions of years. They belong to a group of animals called ungulates (UN-gyoo-lutz), because they have hooves. Also in this group are elk, caribou, whitetail deer, and reindeer. They all are even-toed mammals. That means each hoof has two large toes and two small toes. Humans are odd-toed mammals because we have five toes on each foot.

There are seven different types of moose. Four types are found only in North America, two in Asia, and one in Europe. Scientists who study animals are called zoologists (zoe-OL-uh-jists). They have given every known animal a scientific name. The scientific name for moose is *Alces alces* (AL-sees, AL-sees).

Moose
FUNFACT:

A moose's two small toes are called dew claws.

Moose are usually shy animals, and prefer to stay
hidden in the forest, in winter and summer.

The word "moose" comes from the Algonquin Indians. These were native people who lived throughout the northern regions of Canada. The Algonquins called this strange-looking creature *mooswa*. It means "twig-eater" or "the animal that strips bark off of trees." Early explorers heard this word and through the years, it eventually changed into "moose."

For the Algonquins, the moose was an important animal. It supplied them with food and other things for their survival. Moose meat was a source of nourishment during the long winters. The hide was used to make clothing and provide shelter. And moose bones and antlers were shaped into useful tools.

To find enough food and the right kind of food,
a moose may begin the search very early in the morning.

Even young moose have learned to be on the alert for danger that might be nearby.

When early explorers first came to North America, the moose's range extended as far south as what is now the state of Virginia. Moose proved to be a valuable food source for those early settlers. Unfortunately, as a result, moose were hunted to near extinction along the Atlantic coast.

Today, moose populations are growing, and they can be found throughout every province of Canada and many areas in the United States. These include the states of Idaho, Montana, New Hampshire, North Dakota, Vermont, Wisconsin, and Wyoming. The largest concentrations of moose are in Alaska, Maine, Michigan, and Minnesota.

The area where a moose lives and feeds is called its home range. Zoologists have estimated that a single moose needs about 4 square miles (6.5 square kilometers) of forest or pasture-land in order to survive. Some moose have much larger ranges. If there is plenty of food in a particular area, moose stay within that area. If the food supply runs out, they move to other locations to obtain the food they need. It is not unusual for moose to live their whole lives within a 10-mile (16 kilo-meters) radius.

Moose
FUNFACT:

There are about 80,000 moose in the lower 48 U.S. states, 175,000 in Alaska, and 800,000 in Canada.

Winter can be a difficult time for moose.
But if there is a good supply of food, they will find it.

It is not unusual for older, healthy cows to have twin babies. Sometimes they even have triplets.

Although the moose truly is one of Nature's strangest-looking creatures, its design is well suited for living in its northern habitat.

The first thing you notice about a moose is its large body. It can be as long as 10 feet (3.5 meters). Some moose measure as tall as 7 feet (2.14 meters) at the shoulder.

Female moose are called cows, and may weigh as much as 800 pounds (364 kilograms). Males are called bulls, and may weigh between 900 and 1,800 pounds (410 to 810 kilograms). That would be equal to having about 25 of your friends standing in the same place at the same time!

Moose have very long legs. When you look closely, you'll notice something else very interesting about them. Most four-legged animals have legs that are all the same length. But the moose's front legs are actually longer than its back legs. If a moose takes a drink from the edge of a pond or stream, it may kneel on its front legs to reach the water.

Moose are not jumpers. They prefer to walk around or just step over something in the way. But a moose's long legs allow it to easily walk in very deep snow and wade through ponds and streams. Its long legs keep its belly about 40 inches (103 centimeters) off the ground. You could probably walk right under a moose!

Another feature you'll notice about a moose is its very large nose. It also has a "beard" that hangs from its chin. This flap of skin covered with hair is called a dewlap, or bell. Both bulls and cows have one. Even a baby moose, called a calf, has a very short one. An adult's dewlap is about 8 to 10 inches (20 to 26 centimeters) long. Dewlaps tend to be longer on males than on females.

Zoologists aren't exactly sure about the purpose of the dewlap. Some believe it is used to spread scent, or odor, during mating.

Moose
FUNFACT:

The moose is the largest member of the deer family. Some people know it by its nickname "Old Bucketnose."

The long and thick dewlap helps tell that this is
an older bull in very good health.

To hear better, moose can move one ear at a time.
To see better, they can move one eye at a time.

The coat of a moose is very dark brown. It is made up of hairs called guard hairs, which can measure up to 10 inches (25.4 centimeters) long. And believe it or not, these hairs are hollow. The air trapped inside is warmed by the moose's body heat to insulate it against the cold weather.

The hollow hair also helps the moose float when it swims across a lake or pond.

In the fall, moose grow a layer of thick fur under the guard hairs to help with winter insulation. Each spring, moose shed this layer to be cooler for the summer.

A calf quickly learns to keep up with its mother, on land and in the water.

At first glance a moose seems awkward. But it can run very fast. A moose may need to run to escape predators, or enemies, like black bears, grizzly bears, and wolves.

It is not unusual for a frightened moose to gallop at speeds up to 35 mph (56 kph). That's the average speed limit for cars on many city streets.

Most of the time, however, moose are content to wander peacefully and quietly through their habitat searching for food.

Moose are mostly solitary creatures. They prefer to live and eat by themselves. As a result, moose are rarely found in groups, or herds. When they do get together, it's only because several moose have discovered a good feeding area at the same time. When the food is gone, the moose go off by themselves to find other food sources.

With no predator in sight, this moose should be able to eat and drink in safety.

Zoologists believe that moose eat water plants because they contain large amounts of sodium, or salt, which the moose needs in its diet.

Some animals migrate, or travel, from one location to another. They do this to breed or look for food. Animals such as caribou and elk are known for traveling long distances. Moose are closely related to these species (SPEE-sees), or kinds, of migrating animals.

But moose do not migrate. It would be safe to say that moose wander rather than migrate. That means they go wherever the food is. In summer they may wander up into the mountains. In fall they may wander down to heavily forested areas. They have no preferred routes or territories—they simply look for the best way to the best feeding areas.

Most people eat many different kinds of food. These may include fruits, vegetables, bread, meat, and fish. Humans are omnivores (OM-ni-vorz) because they eat both plants and meat. Moose, however, are herbivores (HERB-uh-vorz) because they eat only plants.

When moose are in lakes or swampy areas they prefer to eat plants such as water lilies, pond weeds, sedges, and eelgrass. In forested areas moose eat leaves, buds, twigs, and bark from white birch, balsam fir, willow, and aspen trees. Other plants eaten by moose include honeysuckle flowers and cranberry bushes. Moose will eat almost any type of plant food!

Moose
FUNFACT:

Moose can reach and feed
on plants 10 feet (3.05 meters)
above the ground. That's the
height of a basketball hoop.

It is rare for two bulls to bed down this close to each other.
They usually prefer to be alone.

Sometimes a moose can't reach up to a high branch on a small tree, or sapling. Instead, the moose straddles the tree and slowly walks forward. This bends the tree down so the moose can eat the hard-to-reach buds and leaves.

A moose only has incisors, or middle teeth, on its bottom jaw. This means it must use its tongue against the roof of its mouth to strip or tear the food off the plant rather than biting it off. Eating this way causes the branches and stems to look ragged. Moose do have back teeth on the upper and lower jaws for grinding the food. They are called molars.

Scientists have estimated that moose may eat as many as 57 different kinds of trees, shrubs, and plants.

In winter, moose must often paw the ground with their sharp hooves to find vegetation under the snow.

Moose must have the right kind of stomach to digest their food. Like cattle, moose are cud chewers. After they eat, they often find a quiet place to rest and bring their food back up to chew it again. After moose swallow their cud for the last time, it moves into a different chamber of the stomach to finish digesting.

Because of their large size, full-grown moose need to eat about 45 pounds (20 kilograms) of food each day. If the food is not very nutritious, like tree bark, they may need to eat even more. People eat only about 3 pounds (1 kilogram) of food each day.

On most days, a moose wakes up just before dawn. It usually feeds until the middle of the morning. Then, it lies down at the edge of a field or meadow in its safe and hidden bedding area. Here it can rest and listen for any predators that might be nearby. After four or five hours, it gets up and feeds until dark. Then, it lies down again in its bed for the night. Moose are diurnal (die-YER-nul), meaning that they are mostly active during the day.

Moose
FUNFACT:

Antlers that have fallen to the ground are often eaten for their calcium by mice.

Pages 30-31: A young female moose often chooses a home range near her mother. But a young male usually travels far away to find his own home range.

In the summer months, moose spend a lot of time in ponds or lakes. Two good reasons are to cool off and to escape biting flies in the forest. Another reason is to eat any water plants that are available.

In fact, a moose may spend an entire day grazing on plants that grow in the shallow water. Or, a moose can dive below the surface—even to a depth of 20 feet (6.1 meters)—to find other tasty pond weeds to eat.

Using special valves in its nostrils, a moose can close its nose. It can then stay underwater for up to 60 seconds while it feeds.

A moose is a very strong swimmer. It often chooses to swim across a lake rather than walk around it. And it can easily swim into deeper water to find pond weeds. A moose can also use the water to escape predators.

With its powerful legs a moose can swim along at a speed of about 6 mph (9 kph). That's faster than in many human swimming races! Even more amazing is the fact that moose have been observed swimming for distances of up to 12 miles (19 kilometers) without stopping.

Moose
FUNFACT:

The moose is the official state animal of Maine. It can also be found on stamps in Sweden and on coins in Canada.

In the spring when antlers are just beginning to grow,
they look like big bumps on the moose's forehead.

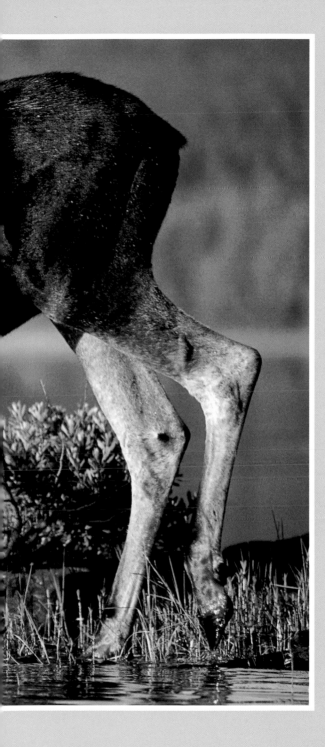

Moose have two very good senses. Their very large ears help moose have good hearing. In fact, a moose could hear a human voice more than a mile away. And with such a big nose, the moose's sense of smell is excellent. Their eyesight isn't as good. But since their eyes are on the sides of their head they can see objects all around them.

If you live in the north you may have seen a moose or two. If not, you can always check the ground for signs of moose. One of the first things to look for is moose tracks. They look like two teardrops side by side. Each track is about 6 inches (15 centimeters) long and 4 inches (11 centimeters) wide. The narrow, sharper end of each track points in the direction the moose was traveling.

The front hooves on a moose are longer than the back ones. The hooves of bulls are longer than those of cows. Scientists have learned that moose usually walk on the tips of their toes. This helps them be quiet while moving through the forest.

When locating moose, you can also look for moose droppings, called scat. Moose droppings are brown and shaped like very large grapes. They are usually in clusters of about twenty-five. In the winter, a moose's droppings are dry and odorless. That's because it mostly eats woody twigs and bark, called browse (BROWZ). In the summer, when a moose eats softer and fresher plants, its droppings are softer and have a slight odor.

This pile of fresh scat is a good clue that a moose was recently in the area. Nearby tracks could show which way it was traveling.

These two bulls are sparring to test each other. One has already lost most of its antler velvet.

If you see moose antlers, you are sure to remember them!

Antlers are made mostly of calcium, and only male moose grow them. Antlers can weigh from about 60 to 85 pounds (27 to 39 kilograms). An average set grows to be approximately 50 inches (127 centimeters) wide. The widest set on record belongs to an Alaskan moose that had antlers 77 inches (186 centimeters) wide.

Because a moose is so tall, the top of its antlers might be over 8 feet (2.5 meters) above the ground.

Antler growth begins in early April. Two tiny antler buds begin to form on the moose's head between its eyes and ears. As the antlers grow, they receive nourishment from a covering of soft, fuzzy skin called velvet.

Antlers continue to grow throughout the spring and summer months. By the middle of August, the antlers are fully grown. It is then that they begin to ossify, or harden. Usually by late August or early September the velvet starts to dry and peels off the antlers. It is during this time that you see moose rubbing their antlers against bushes and trees to scrape off any remaining velvet. When the growth process is completed in late September a moose's antlers are whitish, smooth, and shiny.

Just as no two people have the same set of fingerprints, no two sets of antlers are exactly alike. In fact, one of the ways zoologists can identify an individual moose is by the shape and size of its antlers. Each moose may have a different number of tines, or points, on its antlers. Some are tall and thin, while others are short and wide.

Moose
FUNFACT:

One town in Alaska has a celebration called The Moose Dropping Festival, where you may see many things made out of moose scat—even a necklace!

The bigger the diameter of the antler near the head, the older the moose.
This is an old bull, spreading its legs to reach the water.

Sometimes the antlers are bloody when the velvet comes off, but it doesn't hurt the moose.

The size of the antlers may also indicate the age of a moose. Young bulls begin growing antlers in their first year. This first set is only about 6 to 10 inches (15 to 25 centimeters) long. The following year the antlers grow larger and develop more tines on each side.

The growth process continues every year until the moose is about six years old. Then the antlers are at their full size.

Bulls cast, or shed, their antlers once a year in November or December. Sometimes they drop off together and sometimes they drop off one at a time. Usually both antlers have fallen within a few hours of each other. It doesn't hurt the bull, and new ones begin to grow in the spring.

Most of the time, moose are very quiet animals. They make very few noises. Usually, when a moose makes a sound it is because the moose is in trouble, scared, or injured. At those times, the sound is like high-pitched dog barking. Baby moose call to their mothers by whining like a frightened puppy or bleating like a sheep.

Moose also call to each other during the mating season, called the rut. Cows call with a long, quivering moan that ends in a sound like a cough, "moo-agh!" Then, the bull answers her with a deep, coarse grunt or loud bellow. These sounds often echo across the landscape for long distances. The sound of several males and females calling back and forth to each other makes lots of noise!

Early fall means the start of the rut. During this time of year, adult bulls often challenge each other for the right to mate with a cow. Two bulls may charge each other to prove which one is the strongest. They push and shove until one surrenders and gallops away. Sometimes, when their antlers jam together, the tips may be broken off or the moose may be injured.

The winner of the shoving contest is the one that gets to mate with the female. Most bulls become interested in one cow at a time. But in Alaska, bulls often gather a group of about ten cows, called a harem. The bull stays and mates with these females for about ten days before he moves on to gather another group.

Moose
FUNFACT:

People often enter contests to find out who can best imitate a bull's bellow.

This is called a "lipcurl." It helps the bull find a cow for mating during the rut.

Newborn calves rely on their mother's milk for their first four months. Then they begin to learn which plant foods are good to eat.

The cow chooses a safe and hidden place for her calf to be born. It is usually away from any other moose. Most calves are born in May or June. They have a reddish-brown coat and dark rings around the eyes. A newborn moose weighs about 25 pounds (11.4 kilograms). A calf can usually stand and walk a day or two later. In a few more days, it can even swim.

A moose calf grows fast! For the first few months it may gain as much as 5 pounds (2.25 kilograms) every day. By the time it is one year old, it weighs about 500 pounds (225 kilograms).

A moose calf stays with its mother through the first winter and into the following spring. During this time the mother and calf stay close together. Most of the time, they are only a few yards or meters apart. The mother teaches the calf where to find food and how to avoid predators. Then, she chases the young moose away. When a baby moose is just one year old, it goes out into the world on its own.

If a moose is able to survive the first 2 years of its life, it usually lives to be about 10 years old. Some may live to be 20 years old. Their northern habitat is often harsh and dangerous, but these strange-looking animals have learned to survive very well.

Moose
FUNFACT:

When a calf is one year old, it is called a yearling.

Internet Sites

You can find out more interesting information about moose and lots of other wildlife by visiting these Internet sites.

www.animal.discovery.com   Discovery Channel Online

www.kidsplanet.org   Defenders of Wildlife

www.nationalgeographic.com/kids   National Geographic Society

www.nwf.org/kids   National Wildlife Federation

www.wwf.org   World Wildlife Fund

http://nature.org/   The Nature Conservancy

Index

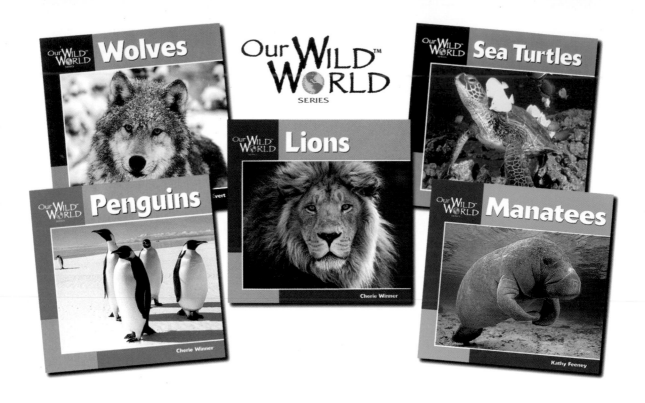

BISON
ISBN 1-55971-775-0
BLACK BEARS
ISBN 1-55971-742-4
CARIBOU
ISBN 1-55971-812-9
CHIMPANZEES
ISBN 1-55971-845-5
COUGARS
ISBN 1-55971-788-2
DOLPHINS
ISBN 1-55971-776-9
EAGLES
ISBN 1-55971-777-7
GORILLAS
ISBN 1-55971-843-9

LEOPARDS
ISBN 1-55971-796-3
LIONS
ISBN 1-55971-787-4
MANATEES
ISBN 1-55971-778-5
MONKEYS
ISBN 1-55971-849-8
MOOSE
ISBN 1-55971-744-0
ORANGUTANS
ISBN 1-55971-847-1
PENGUINS
ISBN 1-55971-810-2
POLAR BEARS
ISBN 1-55971-828-5

SEA TURTLES
ISBN 1-55971-746-7
SEALS
ISBN 1-55971-826-9
SHARKS
ISBN 1-55971-779-3
TIGERS
ISBN 1-55971-797-1
WHALES
ISBN 1-55971-780-7
WHITETAIL DEER
ISBN 1-55971-743-2
WOLVES
ISBN 1-55971-748-3

See your nearest bookseller, or order by phone 1-800-328-3895

NORTHWORD PRESS
Chanhassen, Minnesota